Open

A ZEBRA BOOK
By Sue Tarsky
Illustrated by Deborah Ward

PUBLISHED BY
WALKER BOOKS
LONDON

Open the door. Look inside.
What can you find to eat?

Open the door. Look inside.

What is in the kitchen cupboard?

Open the door.
Look inside.
What do you use
to clean the floor?

Open the door. Look inside.
What belongs in the bathroom?

Open the basket. Look inside.
What needs washing?

Open the drawer. Look inside.
What do you put on your feet?

Open the wardrobe.
Look inside.
What can you wear?

Open the box. Look inside.
What do you dress up in?

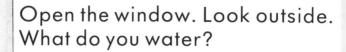
Open the window. Look outside.
What do you water?

Open the door.
Look inside.
What keeps you
dry in the rain?

Open the door. Go outside.

What do you ride?

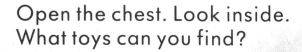

Open the chest. Look inside.
What toys can you find?

Open the box. Look inside.
What a surprise!